David Fickling Books

Dedicated to Team DFB!

The comics in this book were originally published as
Bunny vs Monkey: Destructo and *Bunny vs Monkey: Apocalypse*.

Adaptation, additional artwork and colours by Sammy Borras.
Cover design by Paul Duffield.

Bunny vs Monkey and the League of Doom
is A DAVID FICKLING BOOK

First published in Great Britain in 2021 by
David Fickling Books,
31 Beaumont Street,
Oxford,
OX1 2NP

David Fickling Books reg. no. 8340307

A CIP catalogue record for this book is available from the British Library.

Printed by Grafostil, Slovenia.

Papers used by David Fickling Books are from well-managed forests and other responsible sources.

JAMIE SMART'S

BUNNY
vs
MONKEY

AND THE LEAGUE OF DOOM!

"GROSS!"

IT SURE HAS BEEN QUIET WITHOUT SKUNKY AROUND.

WE USED TO CAUSE MAGNIFICENT HAVOC TOGETHER.

WE'D DESTROY, IN HIS OCTO-BLIVION! CRUSH, IN HIS FROG-O-SAURUS! CRASH, IN THE MOLE-A-ROLLA!

NOW LOOK AT ME. JUST A LONELY MONKEY, POKING SOME MUD WITH A STICK.

4

6

7

8

9

11

18

NONE OF YOU **FEAR** ME ANY MORE! NOT NOW I'M ON MY OWN. I HAD TO PRETEND TO BE A **NEW BADDIE**, SOMEONE REALLY SCARY. I THOUGHT **HE** MIGHT GET YOUR RESPECT!

IT'S NOT BEEN THE SAME SINCE SKUNKY LEFT.

BUT I'LL SHOW YOU! ONE DAY I'LL **RULE** THESE WOODS, AND I'LL MAKE ALL OF YOU SISSIES **DANCE!** Y'HEAR ME? **DANCE!**

DANCE?

DANCE!

GO HOME, MONKEY. STOP TRYING TO CAUSE TROUBLE.

NEVER! I WILL **NEVER** STOP!

I WILL STRIKE AGAIN WHEN YOU **LEAST EXPECT IT!** IN WAYS YOU **COULDN'T POSSIBLY IMAGINE!**

NEXT DAY...

I AM THE **METAL MONKEY!** AND I AM HERE TO **DESTR—**

GO HOME, MONKEY.

SAMLE.

UMM...YES? WHY NOT. LET'S GO WITH THAT.

WE BOW TO YOU, OH, BIG FAT-HEAD SKUNKY!

I COULD GET USED TO THIS.

LESS OF THE 'FAT-HEAD' THOUGH.

I'LL GO AND GET BUNNY! HE'LL BE **AMAZED!**

WHAT? NO! DON'T GET BUNNY! HE'LL WORK OUT HOW I'M DOING THIS!

WELL, IT'S OBVIOUSLY SOME KIND OF **HOLOGRAM!**

AWWW.

I **TOLD** YOU HE'D WORK IT OUT.

NO MATTER! I GAVE YOU ALL A CHANCE TO LEAVE THESE WOODS, BUT YOU HAVEN'T. SO NOW, YOU WILL ALL **SUFFER MY WRATH!**

HANG ON.

IF THIS IS A HOLOGRAM, IS THE **ACTUAL** SKUNKY FILMING THIS FROM INSIDE THAT BIG TEMPLE WE FOUND OVER THE HILL?

YES. I MEAN, NO!

I KNEW IT. I **KNEW** THAT'S WHERE YOU'VE BEEN HIDING!

26

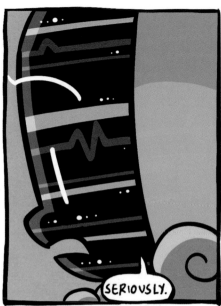

28

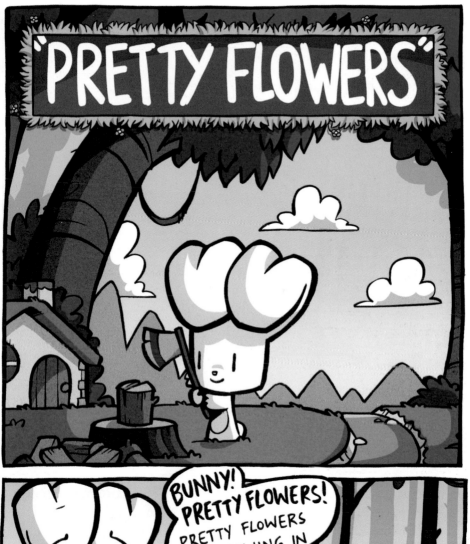

YES, I AM.

I AM **NOT** SURPRISED.

WELL, I DID WARN YOU ALL, BUT YOU DIDN'T LISTEN. NOW I'M **TERRAFORMING**, COVERING THESE WOODS WITH **MONSTROUS PANSIES!**

HAR HAR!

YOU MAY HAVE PIG, BUT YOU'LL NEVER CATCH ME OR WEENIE!

OH, I PROBABLY WILL.

TO BE FAIR, WEENIE'S KINDA A GIVEN.

I THINK **THIS** FLOWER IS SAFE, BUNNY. IT MUST BE, IT'S THE PRETTIEST.

CHOMP!

GRAB!

32

"ALAN"

I AM **A.L.A.N.**, THE ARMOURED LOCATING ARMADILLO NETWORK. A MECHANISED BOUNTY HUNTER WHO KNOWS NO FEAR!

I'M PIG, AND I'M EATING **ICE CREAM.**

CHOOM!

DON'T WORRY, PIG! I CAUGHT HIM IN A **PILLOWCASE!**

SHOOM!

FWOOM!

ERK!

35

GASP! HE'S RIGHT! WE CAN'T PROTECT THE WOODS LIKE THIS!

WE NEED TO **GET FIT**! AND TO DO THAT, WE'LL NEED SOMEONE TO TRAIN US WITH **NO MERCY**!

HELLO? LE FOX? WE NEED YOUR HELP!

MOI? PAH, WHY WOULD YOU NEED ME? I WORK ALONE.

WE'VE ALL LET OURSELVES GET **UNFIT**!

THE STATE WE'RE IN, MONKEY COULD JUST ROLL US DOWN A HILL!

HMM, HE WOULD ENJOY THAT. AND I **REFUSE** TO LET MONKEY HAVE ANY FUN!

VERY WELL, I WILL HELP. BUT MY EXERCISE REGIME WILL BE RUTHLESS!

41

44

46

48

49

51

"BOBBLES"

A BEAUTIFUL METEOR SHOWER FILLS THE NIGHT SKY, BUT ONE LONELY SOUL ISN'T ENJOYING IT.

SIGHH...

I'M THE SADDEST CLOWN IN THE WHOLE UNIVERSE.

I THOUGHT IT WOULD BE FUN TO DRESS UP.

BOBBLES THE CLOWN!

HERE TO CHEER EVERYONE UP!

I FORGOT THAT WEENIE IS TERRIFIED OF CLOWNS...

SCREEEAM! IT'S A GHOSTLY IMP!

AND SO IS BUNNY...

WHAT **ARE** YOU?

DID WE DO SOMETHING BAD?

AND MONKEY JUST GOT VERY ANGRY...

ARE YOU AN **ALIEN?**

GERROFF, THIS IS **MY** PLANET.

IN FACT, EVERYONE TURNED AGAINST ME AND CHASED ME AWAY.

THROW SHOES AT IT!

WE DON'T WEAR SHOES!

AND SO NOW HERE I AM, ALL ALONE UNTIL MY FACEPAINT COMES OFF...

54

"THE TEMPLE"

THERE IT IS! THE TEMPLE WHERE SKUNKY NOW LIVES...

...HIS NEW, SUPER-SECRET LABORATORY!

AND IF PIG HAD REMEMBERED TO BRING THE BINOCULARS, I WOULDN'T BE LOOKING AT IT THROUGH TWO **TOILET ROLLS**.

I THOUGHT THOSE WERE BINOCCLERS.

NO MATTER! WE CAME HERE TO SNEAK INSIDE, TO INFILTRATE SKUNKY'S INGENIOUS SECURITY SYSTEM, AND FIND OUT WHAT'S GOING ON IN THERE.

YAYYY! CHARGE!! CHARRRGE!

NO! QUIETLY!

SHH! SHH!

59

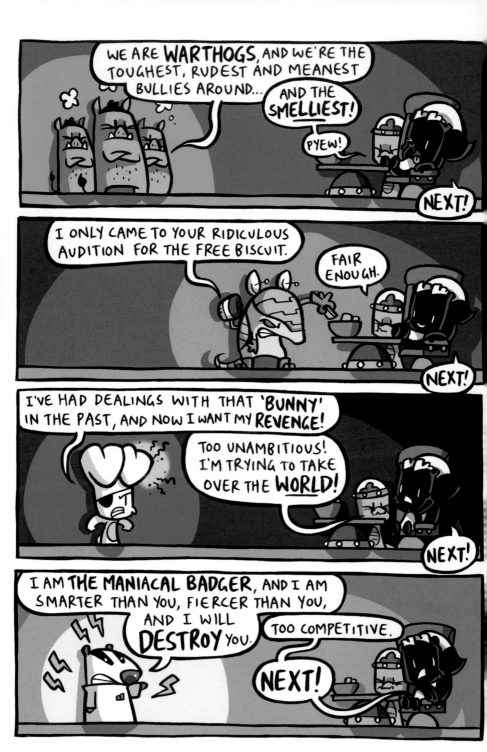

62

RRGH!! EVERY EVIL GENIUS NEEDS AN EVIL GANG TO CARRY OUT HIS EVIL WHIMS.

BUT GETTING A GANG TOGETHER IS HARDER THAN IT LOOKS!

AHEM!

I'M MONK... MICKEY... MIKEY! I'M MIKEY! AND I'M A SUPER TOUGH GUY! GRRR!

SIGHHH. MONKEY, THAT'S YOU.

WHO IS THIS 'MONKEY'? I'M MIKEY! I'LL FIGHT EVERYONE!

MONKEY, YOU'RE HOLDING UP THE AUDITION.

BUT HOW DID YOU KNOW IT WAS MEEEE? I'M WEARING THIS AMAZING DISGUISE!

OH, Y'KNOW.

JUST A HUNCH.

PLEEEEEASE LET ME JOIN YOUR EVIL GANG, SKUNKY! OH PLEASE OH PLEASE OH PLEASE! I'M SO EVIL!

NO, YOU'RE AN IDIOT. YOU ALWAYS RUIN EVERYTHING!

I DON'T! I DON'T!

TO BE IN MY GANG, YOU NEED TO BE A REAL VILLAIN. STRONG, MEAN, AND COOL.

LIKE, UM...

LIKE...

IS...
...IS **THAT** THE TOILET?

HOW DO I SIT ON IT?

AH, PIGULUS, YOU'VE FOUND MY LATEST **TERRIFYING WEAPON!**

AND I MUST SAY, IT'S LUCKY YOU'RE ALREADY WEARING A HELMET!

I CALL THIS THE **BOOM BOOM!** A HUGE CANNON, PRIMED AND READY TO DESTROY HUGE CHUNKS OF THE WOODS!

COME AND SEE!

68

CRUNCH!

TIMBERRR!

MY HOUSE!

PFFT, WHATEVER. I SUPPOSE THIS **IS** QUITE EVIL.

BUT LOOK! I HAVE A SCARY **HAND-PUPPET**, AND IT'S **SCARING WEENIE!**

BOOOO!

SERIOUSLY?

YES!

I AM USING THE REMAINING **ROCKET FUEL** FROM MY CRAFT TO BLOW UP RANDOM THINGS!

WHEEE!

BOOM!

YEAH? WELL, I JUST TRICKED BUNNY INTO WALKING IN A BIT OF DOG POO! HAHA!

EURGH.

THIS WAY TO CAKES →

LISTEN, LESS EVIL MONKEY, YOU'RE NOT EVIL AT ALL. YOU'RE JUST ANNOYING.

IT'S NOT MY FAULT, I DON'T HAVE THE RIGHT TOOLS! NOT SINCE SKUNKY LEFT.

WELL, I'M HERE NOW, SO YOU CAN JUST GO AWAY!

THIS ISN'T FAIR! I'M STILL AN EVIL MONKEY AT HEART!

...IE DAY, I'LL STILL DESTROY THIS PLACE!

I MEAN, LOOK AT MY OPPOSITION! THEY'RE SO **STUPID!**

GASP!

GASP!

I MAY BE THE MOST CRUEL AND EVIL MONKEY IN THE UNIVERSE, BUT I WOULDN'T GO OUT OF MY WAY TO **HURT SOMEONE'S FEELINGS!**

I'M NOT HANGING AROUND HERE IF YOU'RE GOING TO BE LIKE THAT!

LOOK, I'M SORRY, WEENIE.

NO, NO. YOU'VE SAID IT.

74

MY LATEST INVENTION—THE **GRASSHOPPALONG,** ESCAPED FROM MY LABORATORY!

SO, I THOUGHT, WHAT IS THE BEST THING I COULD INVENT TO CATCH A GIANT INSECT?

A GIANT **TARSIER!** TARSIERS LOVE EATING INSECTS!

MEEP!

THEY CAN ALSO LEAP **INCREDIBLE DISTANCES!**

P- DOINGG!

JUST OVER THE HILL...

WHAT A LOVELY DAY FOR A PICNIC! IF ONLY I WAS SHARING IT WITH SOMEONE.

DOOF!

SHRIEK! NOT YOU! **NOT YOU!**

A LITTLE FURTHER ROUND THE CORNER...

I THINK I'LL HAVE A PICNIC TODAY!

BUT I'LL EAT ALL THE NICE CAKES BEFORE I INVITE...

DOOF!

AIIIEE! HAVE THE CAKES! HAVE THEM!

SKUNKY, YOUR TARSIER IS DOING FAR MORE DAMAGE THAN YOUR GRASSHOPPER.

GRASSHOPPALONG! THERE IT IS!

HOP! HOP! HOP!

B-YOOIING!

AND BESIDES, A TARSIER ISN'T THE BEST IDEA FOR AN INVENTION. IT SAYS HERE THEY'RE **NOCTURNAL**.

THEY **SLEEP** IN THE **DAY**.

BIG BOOK OF ANIMALS

76

"UNCLE FOX"

HAR HAR HARR! COME, MY **LEAGUE OF DOOM!** RIDE WITH ME IN MY **DOOMOBILE!!**

BRUMMM!!

EV1L

WE'LL HEAD OVER TO BUNNY'S HOUSE, AND FILL IT WITH **CUSTARD!**

BZZT! I DETECT THAT SOMETHING IS FOLLOWING US!

HMM. I DETECT IT TOO.

79

I MUST PROTECT BUNNY AND HIS FRIENDS! I HAVE WRONGED THEM IN ZE PAST.

WELL, MAYBE I CAN HELP, EH? I DID USED TO BE QUITE THE **SUPERSPY** BACK IN MY DAY.

WHY, I SINGLE-HANDEDLY BROUGHT DOWN THE NAZIS WHILE DRESSED AS A PANDA!

I CAN'T REMEMBER WHY I WAS DRESSED LIKE THAT, TO BE HONEST.

THERE'S NO NEED TO MAKE UP STORIES JUST TO IMPRESS **ME**, UNCLE.

AW, OKAY.

I NEED TO FIND A WAY TO STOP **SKUNKY.** HE'S ALREADY RUN ME OVER ONCE TODAY.

WELL, YOU KNOW WHAT WE FOXES SAY?

TWO FOXES ARE ONE MORE FOX THAN ONE FOX.

UMM... I

WELL, I THOUGHT, IF I'M GOING TO BE EVIL I MAY AS WELL MAKE SOME MONEY AT IT.

SO NOW I'M IN THE **PROPERTY** MARKET!

YOU BUILT A HOUSE HERE **JUST** TO ANNOY ME?

YES! WELL, YOU SAY "HOUSE", IT'S MADE OUT OF CARDBOARD AND CHEWING GUM, BUT DON'T TELL OUR NEW TENANT THAT.

BUT I LIKE MY PRIVACY.

WINK!

I'LL LEAVE YOU TWO TO GET ALONG, THEN. HAR HAR!

OH, ARE THOSE FOR ME?

CHOMP!

LOVELY.

I SUPPOSE, PERHAPS, HAVING A NEIGHBOUR WOULDN'T BE TOO BAD. WE MIGHT GET ALONG!

DUH-DUHH DUHDUHDUH WEEOWEEE!

ARGH! WE'RE **NEVER** GOING TO GET ALONG!

86

"THE TRUCE!"

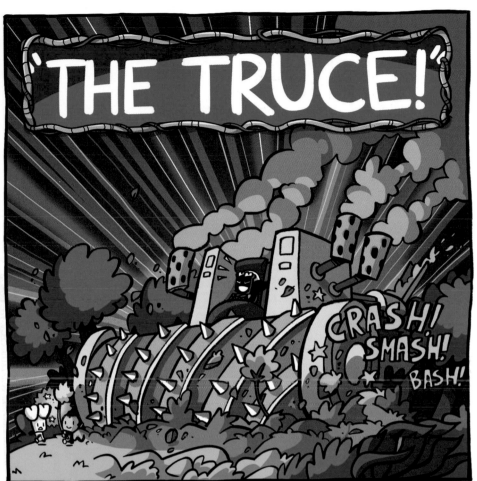

CRASH! SMASH! BASH!

MONKEY, THIS IS NOT THE TIME TO BE HITTING ME WITH A TREE BRANCH!

EVERY TIME IS THE TIME!

THWACK!

WE'RE ABOUT TO BE MOWN DOWN BY SKUNKY'S DE-FORESTER 9000!!

IT ADDS DRAMA!

THWACK!

CHUK!
CHUK!
CHUK!
THPTHBTHH!

AWW.

PROBABLY JUST THE FAN BELT. I'LL HAVE THIS FIXED IN A JIFFY — CAN YOU STAY THERE WHILE I DO?

I'D RATHER NOT, TO BE HONEST.

WELL, WHILE WE'RE WAITING...

THWACK!

MONKEY! SERIOUSLY!

DON'T YOU GET IT? WE'RE **ALL** IN DANGER FROM SKUNKY, EVEN **YOU**. WE CAN ONLY FIGHT BACK IF WE WORK TOGETHER!

BUT... BUT THWACK?

88

94

95

"SKI-DADDLE!"

99

100

MEANWHILE, AT THE LEAGUE OF DOOM SECRET H.Q....

HAR HAR HAR! MY PLAN IS GOING PERFECTLY!

IF I CAN'T SCARE THEM OUT OF THE WOODS, I'LL TRICK THEM INTO BEING BRUTALLY HONEST WITH EACH OTHER...

...SO THEY ALL FALL OUT AND WANT TO LEAVE THE WOODS BY THEMSELVES!

BZZT! HERE'S THE **BATTERY** FOR THE TRUTHOMETER, SIR! WHERE DO YOU WANT IT?

GASP!

YOU MEAN...THE TRUTHOMETER DOESN'T HAVE A BATTERY IN IT?!

SO IT'S NOT EVEN WORKING?

THEY'RE JUST TELLING EACH OTHER THE TRUTH BECAUSE THEY THINK IT IS?

THEY'RE FLYING BLIND!

BACK IN THE WOODS...

MONKEY! MONKEY, COME AND HAVE A GO ON THE TRUTHOMETER!

I DON'T HAVE TIME FOR YOUR SILLY TOYS!

I'M A VERY BUSY MONKEY.

OH, DON'T BE A SPOILSPORT!

THIS IS OUR CHANCE TO FIND OUT WHAT YOU REALLY THINK!

PLONK!

I'M... I'M NOT SURE THAT'S A GOOD IDEA?

I DESPISE YOU ALL AND I WANT TO TAKE OVER THE WOODS!!

WE KNEW THAT ALREADY!

PFFT! TELL US SOMETHING NEW!

I AM SUPER-MEAN WITH NO MORALS, AND NO LOVE IN MY HEART!

REALLY? THAT'S KINDA SAD.

I AM A FAILURE AT EVERYTHING!

WHOA!

SOMETIMES I GET REALLY LONELY!

I CAN'T SLEEP AT NIGHT WITHOUT MISTER DUCKY!

BOOHOO!

QUACK!

110

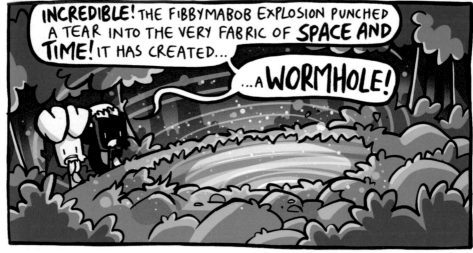

114

118

119

121

WELL, WEENIE AND PIG ARE SPENDING THE DAY EXPLORING THE MORE DANGEROUS PARTS OF THE WOODS.

A BEE! SCREEEAM!

EEE!

AND LE FOX IS SITTING IN A HOLE WITH MUD ON HIS HEAD.

HUMPH.

I CAN'T RECALL WHY.

ANYWAY, THE POINT IS, EVERYONE ELSE IS BUSY.

ALSO, YOU'RE THE ONE WHO HIT ME WITH A SPADE IN THE **FIRST PLACE!**

CLANG!

OW!

HAR HAR!

OH YEAH. HEH HEH HEH...

IT'S NOT FUNNY, MONKEY. YOU NOW HAVE TO LOOK AFTER ME UNTIL I'M ALL BETTER!

IF YOU WANT TO HANG OUT WITH US NOW, YOU SHOULD START BEING NICER.

I DON'T **WANT** TO HANG OUT WITH YOU!

I WANT TO BE...

124

IN SKUNKY'S LAIR...

HEY, WHERE DID MY BOTTLE OF **FART POTION** GO?

FRRPP!

OOH, EXCUSE ME!

A **WHISK**? WHAT'S THAT FOR?

IT'S FOR **LATER.** WHEN WE DO THE **SURGERY.**

THE...WHAT?

FOR NOW, I THINK THIS PATIENT COULD DO WITH SOME FRESH AIR!

WHAT? NO! PUT ME DOWN!

WHEEL!

...AND A **HEDGE!**

OOMF!

SHOVE!

WE'RE BACK!

OH THANK GOODNESS, A **NURSE!**

WE GOT STUNG BY A **BEE!**

HMM, YOU'RE IN LUCK.

125

126

BOOP! BOOP!

GO AWAY! I ALREADY TOLD YOU, YOU'RE A HEALTH HAZARD!

RRGH! I TRIED TO BE AN EVIL TYRANT, BUT NO ONE WOULD LET ME! SO I TRIED TO BE A GOOD GUY, AND I NEARLY DIIIIIIIED OF THE BOREDOM! SO LET ME IN YOUR GANG NOW.

GOT HIM! JUST BEFORE HE HAD THE CHANCE TO GO INSIDE!

THUNK!!

RRFF!

?

PSCHH!

WE'VE BEEN LOOKING FOR YOU FOR A LONGGGG TIME, LITTLE MONKEY.

AND NOW YOU'RE OURS.

THPTHBTHH!

HUMAN BEINGS! THIS FAR INTO THE WOODS?

AND MONKEY'S IMPORTANT TO THEM?

MONKEY'S NOT IMPORTANT TO ANYONE.

I CAN'T LET THEM TAKE HIM! RELEASE... THE CLUCKEN!!

BOO

135

"A NEW HOME"

137

HEE HEE! WHAT ARE YOU? A CAT? A LITTLE BLACK-AND-WHITE KITTY CAT?

NO! I AM THE MOST EVIL SUPER-GENIUS IN THE WORLD!

HEE HEE! WHAT CUTE FRIENDS YOU HAD HERE, STEVE.

NOT CUTE! A SUPER-GENIUS! SUPER-GENIUS!

AND A SKUNK TOO! LOOK!

FRRP! FRRP!

STINK! GUFF!

A WHIFFY SKUNK!

A STINKY, GROSS...

SHE'S GONE, SKUNKY.

BUT... BUT THAT LITTLE GIRL STOLE MY ULTIMATE WEAPON!

WELL, HE SEEMED QUITE HAPPY TO GO WITH HER.

HE DID

BACK IN SKUNKY'S HQ...

MAYBE BUNNY'S RIGHT. MAYBE METAL STEVE DOES DESERVE A BETTER LIFE. MAYBE I SHOULD JUST ACCEPT HE'S GONE.

OR, MAYBE I SHOULD USE HIS REMOTE CONTROL TO RUIN THEIR NEW FRIENDSHIP!

BIT GRUMPY
ANGRY
DESTRUCTO
APOCALYPSE

142

OH, STOP BEING SILLY. A LOT OF US ARE A LITTLE SHORT-SIGHTED.

HERE, TRY ON MY GLASSES.

I CAN SEE!

WELL, GOOD. BUT YOU'RE NOT GETTING BACK ON MY WAHEY-ELL, I DON'T TR—

THAT'S FINE! I DON'T WANT TO ANYWAY!

NOW I CAN SEE PROPERLY, I CAN APPRECIATE ALL THE INCREDIBLE DETAILS OF LIFE! THE INTRICATE TEXTURE OF EXISTENCE!

THERE IS SO MUCH TO SAVOUR AND ENJOY!

THWACK!

OWWW!

HAR! BRILLIANT.

STAY THERE. ONCE MORE.

AWAKE, SLEEPING BUNNY! WE ARE **THE**...

YEAH, ALL RIGHT, I GOT THAT BIT WHY AM I NOT IN MY HOUSE?

WE SNEAKED YOU OUT, TO BRING YOU FAR BELOW GROUND.

RARR!

...TO SEE IF YOU CAN ESCAPE THE **LABYRINTH!**

IF YOU **DO**, YOU MAY STAY IN THE WOODS. IF YOU **DON'T**, WELL, YOU'LL PROBABLY HAVE BEEN FLATTENED OR SOMETHING.

BUT... WHY?

WHY... WHAT?

WHY DO I HAVE TO PLAY THIS SILLY GAME? WHO PUT YOU IN CHARGE?

BECAUSE WE ARE THE ORDER OF THE WOODS!

AND WE HAVE AN **ELECTRIC PROD!**

BZZAP!

YARGH! OKAY, I'M GOING!

I DON'T KNOW WHAT'S GOING ON HERE, BUT IF THERE'S A WAY OUT I'M GUESSING IT'S THIS WAY.

HURRY UP!

THIS WAY

ALONG HERE!

THROUGH HERE.

THIS WAY!

IT IS THIS WAY YES.

147

149

BENEATH THE WAVES

HERE WE ARE, MONKEY! SAT INSIDE MY NEWEST VEHICLE...

...THE W1000 AQUEOUS SUBMERSIBLE!

OR "WASSSUB", FOR SHORT.

WE'RE FULLY EQUIPPED FOR EVERY SITUATION.

LIFE JACKETS, OXYGEN MASKS, SANDWICH DISPENSER, FREE WI-FI...

THAT'S ALL GREAT, BUT...

BEFORE LONG...

CRUMBLE!

WE DID IT!

WE DISCOVERED THE **GREAT LOST LAKE!**

WHATEVER WE DISCOVER DOWN HERE HAS PROBABLY LAIN UNSEEN FOR CENTURIES!

SPLOOSH!

MAYBE LONGER!

HANG ON, DID YOU BUILD A **TOILET** IN THIS THING?

SHUSH, MONKEY! WE ARE **EXPLORING!**

GASP! LOOK, ANCIENT RUINS! ISN'T IT AMAZING?

I NEED THE TOILET.

IT'S **AMAZING.**

IT WON'T BE WHEN IT HAPPENS.

CAN'T I JUST OPEN A WINDOW AND... **EEK!** WHAT WAS THAT?

155

SUPER ACTION BEAVER

ACTION BEAVER, YOU CAN'T GO AROUND DOING THIS! GETTING ALL MUDDY AND RUINING TEA PARTIES!

YOU SHOULD BE CLEAN AND POLITE!

LIKE US!

ACTUALLY, PIG, ARE YOU THINKING WHAT I'M THINKING?

YES. CAN I DRINK LEMONADE THROUGH MY EAR IF I USE A LONG ENOUGH STRAW?

NO, THE OTHER THING I'M THINKING.

WE SHOULD GIVE ACTION BEAVER A MAKE OVER!

A POSH GENTLEMAN!

BARPLE!

OH, HOW CIVILISED!

OR MAYBE A WELL-TO-DO HEIRESS!

HONK!

SHE LOOKS DIVINE!

HMM, I'M NOT SURE WE'RE GETTING TO THE HEART OF WHO ACTION BEAVER REALLY IS.

I HEARD HE DRANK ONE OF SKUNKY'S INVENTIONS AND GOT SUPERPOWERS.

THEN THAT'S IT!

159

"STONE COLD"

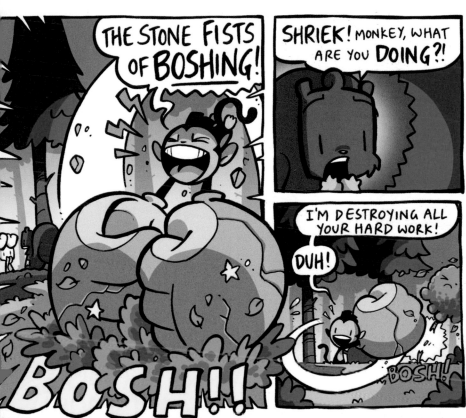

162

THE CRIMSON GOBBLER!

IT COMES AT NIGHT, THAT HIDEOUS BEAST, PROWLING THROUGH THE DARK SKIES...

THEY CALL IT...

THE CRIMSON GOBBLER!

...AND IT KEEPS EATING ALL OUR SOUFFLÉS!

WAIT WAIT WAIT.

WHAT?

SOUFFLÉS! THEY'RE A DELICIOUS EGG-BASED DISH!

THE TRICK IS TO GET A LOT OF AIR IN THE BATTER, MAKING IT LIGHT AND FLUFFY!

IN FACT, I'M **SO GOOD** AT BAKING SOUFFLÉS, I HAVE TO TIE MINE TO A BRANCH TO STOP THEM **FLOATING AWAY!**

BUT THAT... **THING!** IT CAME LAST NIGHT AND **ATE** MY SOUFFLÉS!

I SAW IT! BIG RED FACE!

EEE!

EEE!

I STILL DON'T UNDERSTAND WHY YOU'RE TELLING *ME* ALL THIS.

BECAUSE IT'S *YOU*! OR SOMETHING TO DO WITH *YOU*!

IT'S ALWAYS SOMETHING TO DO WITH YOU!

HOW DARE YOU! I'LL HAVE YOU KNOW, ME AND MY LEAGUE OF DOOM WERE BUSY ALL LAST NIGHT, HAVING A WILD PARTY!!

LAST NIGHT...

BZZT! ACTION BEAVER IS STUCK IN THE TOILET AGAIN.

SIGH. LEAVE HIM.

IT'S THE ONLY WAY HE'LL LEARN.

SO ANYWAY, IT CAN'T HAVE BEEN ME, OR ANY OF MY LEAGUE.

WELL, IT'S HARDLY LIKELY TO HAVE BEEN *BUNNY*, IS IT?

AND WE HAVEN'T SEEN LE FOX FOR WEEKS.

THEN, PERHAPS, IT IS... A REAL MONSTER!

AIIIEE! HOW...

...EXCITING! YES, IT IS!

WEENIE, YOUR NEW BATCH OF SOOOFFLAYS...

...SOUFFLÉS!

WHATEVER.

WE'LL USE THEM AS BAIT! MEET BACK HERE TONIGHT!

AND WE WILL CATCH THE CRIMSON GOBBLER!

167

THE DESTROY-O-TORIUM!

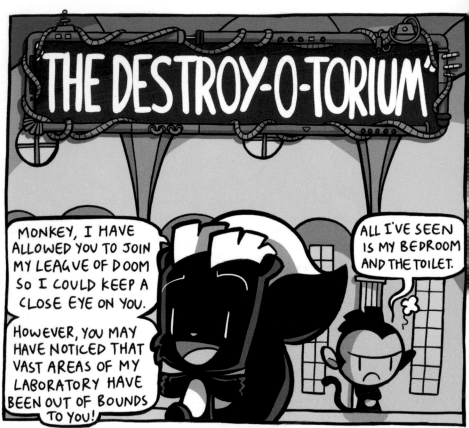

MONKEY, I HAVE ALLOWED YOU TO JOIN MY LEAGUE OF DOOM SO I COULD KEEP A CLOSE EYE ON YOU.

HOWEVER, YOU MAY HAVE NOTICED THAT VAST AREAS OF MY LABORATORY HAVE BEEN OUT OF BOUNDS TO YOU!

ALL I'VE SEEN IS MY BEDROOM AND THE TOILET.

YOUR BEDROOM IS THE TOILET.

BUT NOW, I THINK YOU'RE READY TO EXPERIENCE ALL OF MY SECRETS! TO EXPLORE THE DESTROY-O-TORIUM!

A BOOKCASE?

OH, IT'S NOT ALL IN **BOOKS**, IS IT?

I DON'T HAVE TO REEEEAD?

169

170

171

WELL, HOW ARE YOU GOING TO GET THE SATELLITE DISH BACK ON THE ROOF? YOU'LL **HAVE** TO COME OUTSIDE!

HA!

HMM, HE'S RIGHT...

...UNLESS...

SHRIEK!! THE **CRIMSON GOBBLER** HAS RETURNED!

RUN AWAY!! YEEEARGH!

?

TYING THE SATELLITE DISH TO A KITE AND SAILING IT OUT OF THE CHIMNEY!

INGENIOUS!

THANKS!

BUT NOT AS INGENIOUS AS **ME**, WITH MY INGENIOUS ...

174

175

"MONKEY WITH A FLAME THROWER"

178

181

SKUNKY **FOUND** HIS LABORATORY, HE DID NOT BUILD IT HIMSELF.

SO THE REAL QUESTION YOU SHOULD ALL BE ASKING IS...

WHO DID? AND WHAT EXACTLY WERE THEY TRYING TO DO?

UM...

PERHAPS THERE ARE SECRETS INSIDE THIS LABORATORY OF WHICH EVEN SKUNKY IS UNAWARE?

ERM...

IN PARTICULAR, THERE IS ONE DEVICE EVEN HE MUST NEVER GET HIS HANDS ON.

A MACHINE SO DIABOLICAL, ITS PURPOSE SO HORRIFIC, WE WOULD ALL REGRET HIS EVER FINDING IT!

SO I TOOK THE **BATTERIES** OUT OF IT.

BUZZ!

OOOOOOOOOOOOOH!

NOW GO! RUN BACK TO SAFETY!

AND BE SURE TO TELL BUNNY WHAT I'VE WARNED YOU OF TODAY!

182

183

"MIXEY-MATOSIS"

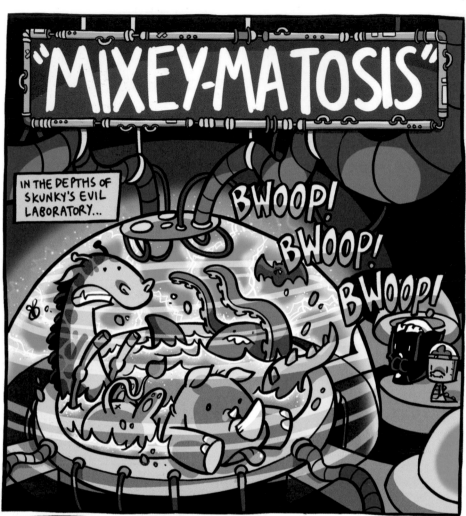

...AN INFLATABLE CHAIR!?!

FRRP!

AUGH! WEENIE, WE AGREED YOU'D BRING A **TENT!**

I MADE AN **EXECUTIVE DECISION!**

RRRRGH!! WHY DID I EVER COME CAMPING WITH YOU TWO?

THE BEAUTY OF NATURE!

BEING AT ONE WITH THE WOODS!

FLUMP!

WE ALL LIVE IN THE WOODS **ANYWAY.**

HUFF!

OWW!

KICK!

WELL, THAT WAS REALLY SILLY, BUNNY. NOW YOU'VE HURT YOUR FOOT.

LET'S JUST GET THE SAUSAGES OUT AND HAVE SOME DINNER.

HOP! HOP!

UMM.

THE... SAUSAGES?

BURP!

WHAT? YOU **ATE** THE SAUSAGES OUT OF MY BAG?

195

THE MONO-CHROMATRON

HANG ON, DID I WAKE UP IN THE OLDEN DAYS?

BUNNY, WE'RE GREY!

WE GOT OLD!

HMM, THAT'S ONE POSSIBILITY. THE OTHER, MORE LIKELY POSSIBILITY, IS THAT SKUNKY HAS DONE SOMETHING TO **SUCK ALL OF THE COLOUR OUT OF THE WORLD!**

WOOD-O-VISION

"SKUNKY DID IT!" MEH MEH MEH! SKUNKY SKUNKY SKUNKY! IT'S ALWAYS **ME** THEY BLAME, ISN'T IT.

VWUP! VWUP! VWUP!

I THOUGHT YOU **DID** DO IT?

WELL, YES, I DID. I JUST RESENT BEING THE FIRST ONE THEY THINK OF.

BUT YOU **WANTED** THEM TO KNOW HOW BRILLIANT YOU ARE!

OH YES, I **DO**.

THAT'S WHY YOU MADE ME WEAR THIS **HAT**.

NOT THE BRILLIANT ONE

YOU'RE RIGHT! AND THE **MONOCHROMATRON** WILL BE THE DEVICE TO PROVE HOW MUCH OF AN EVIL GENIUS I AM!

VWUP!

EVERY BEAUTIFUL COLOUR, STOLEN FROM NATURE, AND CONCEALED INSIDE...

...THIS **EGG**! AND WITH IT, I CAN HOLD THE ENTIRE WORLD TO RANSOM!

PSCHHHH!

BUT FIRST... **TO SHOW OFF ABOUT IT!**

HAR HAR! YOUR PRECIOUS WOODS LOOK A LITTLE **DRAB**, DON'T THEY?

I WONDER WHERE ALL THE PRETTY COLOURS WENT?

TEE HEE!

MEH. WE'RE NOT REALLY BOTHERED, TO BE HONEST.

WHAT? YES YOU ARE!

NAH. WE'RE FINE.

I JUST SUCKED **ALL THE COLOUR** OUT OF THE **WORLD!** DO YOU HAVE ANY IDEA THE KIND OF **GENIUS BRAIN** REQUIRED TO EVEN **CONCEIVE** OF SUCH AN INCREDIBLE IDEA, LET ALONE **ACTUALLY DO IT?**

YOU UNGRATEFUL SWINES!!

NOW, PIG!

SHAKE! SHAKE!

199

I'M TOO BUSY! DO YOU REMEMBER THOSE STRANGE METAL PLATES IN THE GROUND WHICH, WHEN METAL STEVE STOOD ON THEM, TRANSFORMED HIM INTO A **MEGA ROBOT?!**

NO.

NO.

WELL, I WANT HIM TO STAND ON ONE OF THEM AGAIN!

BECAUSE I FOUND HIS INSTRUCTION MANUAL, AND I THINK I CAN OVERRIDE THE ACTIVATION!

PROJECT: METAL STEVE

AND THEN USE HIM TO FIRE **GREAT BIG MISSILES** AT SKUNKY'S LABORATORY!

WHEE!

WHERE DID YOU GET ALL THESE BITS OF METAL FROM?

MY **CAR!**

RANGER

DUNNO. FOUND THEM. **AHA!** WE'RE HERE! EVERYONE GET READY FOR METAL STEVE'S **AMAZING TRANSFORMATION!**

HMM.

DANCE AROUND, METAL STEVE! MAYBE THAT'LL SET IT...

LA LA

LA

LA

VTTTTT!

BZZ!

...OFF!

WHAT DO WE DO NOW, BUNNY?

WHAT NOW?

UMM...UM...PRESS F5 FOR A SYSTEM REBOOT, CTRL+V FOR MANUAL OVERRIDE, SPACE BAR FOR HOT CHOCOLATE..

PRESS EVERYTHING!

EEK!

PROJECT METAL STEVE

BZZZT.

OOPS.

IS THIS ON?

HELLO?

I DON'T HAVE MUCH TIME.

MY NAME IS PROFESSOR SAMUEL P. TINSTONE, AND I'M THE CHIEF SCIENCE OFFICER HERE AT MEANIECORP LABORATORIES.

BOOM!

ARGH!

WE HAVE DONE A TERRIBLE THING HERE.

A TERRIBLE THING!

WE SPENT MANY YEARS EXPERIMENTING, INVENTING, TRYING TO TURN ANIMALS INTO WEAPONS! BUT, IN OUR HASTE, WE ACCIDENTALLY UNLEASHED A CREATURE FROM THE GREAT BELOW!

THE **MOSHOGGOTH** RISES!!!

AND NOW WE ARE EVACUATING, LEAVING THE LABORATORIES TO ROT IN THE WOODS.

HOPING NO ONE WILL UNEARTH OUR SECRET!

I RECORD THIS MESSAGE AS A LAST BROADCAST, SO SHOULD ANYONE UNCOVER IT, HEED MY WARNINGS.

STAY AWAY FROM—

SWOOP!

ARGH!

STOP FILMING, METAL STEVE!

STOP FILM—

LA LA
LA
LA

WEENIE, PIG, LET'S GO AND PLAY HIDE N' SEEK AFTER ALL.

ACTUALLY...

...LET'S JUST PLAY 'HIDE'.

"TO DESTINYYY"

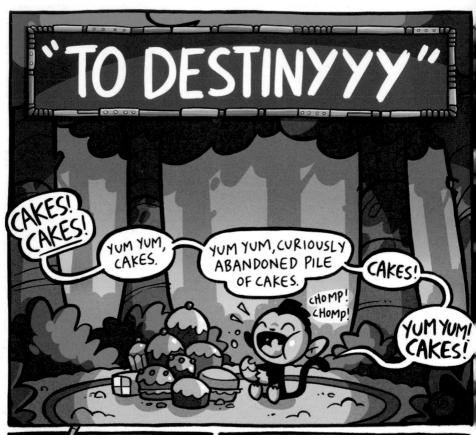

BACK AT THE HEADQUARTERS OF THE BRITISH SPACE PROGRAMME...

WE'VE DONE IT, SIR! THE EXACT MONKEY YOU WANTED!

AND HE ONLY BIT US TWICE!

HEAD OF RESEARCH

YOU DON'T REMEMBER ME, DO YOU?

ARE YOU ON TV? I MOSTLY WATCH MONKEY GAME SHOWS.

OF COURSE. WELL, LITTLE MONKEY, WE HAVE BEEN TRACKING YOU FOR A LONG, LONG TIME.

STORE ROOM

YOU'RE VERY SPECIAL.

YOU ARE GOING TO LEAD US...

...TO GREATNESS!

STORE ROOM

DO NOT TOUCH

IS THIS THE TOILET?

I HOPE SO.

MONKEY, WHAT IS THE THING YOU WANT MOST IN THIS WORLD?

TO DESTROY EVERYTHING OF BEAUTY! TO RULE OVER THE CHARRED REMAINS! TO THROW BIG GLOBS OF MUD AT BUNNY!

OH, AND YOU WILL.

THE NEXT PERSON YOU SEE, GIVE THEM THIS LETTER. AND HAVE A SAFE JOURNEY.

SAFE JOURNEY WHERE?

BWOOOOOOP!

TEN YEARS AGO, ON THE OTHER SIDE OF THE WOODS...

WE'VE DONE IT, SIR! WE'VE INVENTED A TIME MACHINE!

HMM, IT'S GOOD. I SUPPOSE.

CHIEF SCIENCE OFFICE

BUT WHAT I BUILT THIS FACILITY TO DO IS DESTROY EVERYTHING OF BEAUTY. TO RULE OVER THE CHARRED REMAINS!

TO THROW BIG GLOBS OF MUD AT A BUNNY!

"FIND THE MONKEY"

SO!! THIS IS WHAT WE KNOW SO FAR...

SKUNKY'S EVIL LAIR IS **ACTUALLY** THE OLD MEANIECORP BUILDING...

...MEANIECORP CREATED TERRIFYING EXPERIMENTS...

...INCLUDING **METAL STEVE**...

...BUT HAD TO EVACUATE WHEN THEY UNLEASHED A MYSTERIOUS ANCIENT MONSTER CALLED THE **MOSHOGGOTH!**

THIS MEANS SKUNKY IS SITTING ON TOP OF A **GREAT BIG MONSTER**, AND HE DOESN'T EVEN KNOW IT!

YES HE DOES!

SKUNKY! YOU WERE HIDING UNDER A NAPKIN ALL THIS TIME?

I THOUGHT ONE OF YOU MIGHT NOTICE, BUT...

...NOPE.

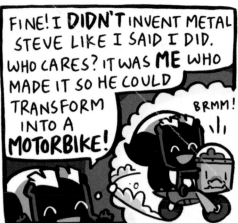

FINE! I **DIDN'T** INVENT METAL STEVE LIKE I SAID I DID. WHO CARES? IT WAS **ME** WHO MADE IT SO HE COULD TRANSFORM INTO A **MOTORBIKE!**

BRMM!

WHO'S COOL? IS IT ME?

IT'S ME! BRUMM!

THE MONSTER, SKUNKY!

THE MOSHOGGOTH!

THPTHBTHH! THAT'S JUST A MYTH. THERE'S NO SUCH THING AS MONSTERS!

APART FROM ALL THE MONSTERS I MAKE.

OBVIOUSLY.

ANYWAY, I CAME ROUND TO ASK IF YOU'VE SEEN MONKEY? HE'S GONE MISSING, AND MY TOILETS WON'T CLEAN THEMSELVES.

WELL, THEY DO, BUT DON'T TELL HIM THAT.

UMM... NO. I HAVEN'T SEEN HIM.

IT'S STARTING TO SNOW OUTSIDE! HE MIGHT BE **COLD!**

209

I'VE BUILT US A **NEW** MONKEY!

TAA-DAA!

THIS MONKEY IS MADE FROM A STRAW-FILLED SACK. ALSO, HE DOESN'T FART OR ANSWER BACK!

GASP! HE'S PERFECT!

HAR HAR! ARE YOU SERIOUS? I COULD CONSTRUCT A **FAR** BETTER MONKEY, MERELY BY USING HIS DNA...

MONKEY THINKS YOU'RE A RUDE SHOW-OFF!!

CLONK!

YARGH!

RETREAT! **RETREAT!** THIS MONKEY'S **FAR** MORE DANGEROUS THAN THE REAL ONE!

BOO HOO HOO!

JAMIE

I MUST PLACE A SAUCER OF MILK, AND THE SECRET SCHEMATICS FOR **THE MOST DEVASTATING WEAPON THE WORLD HAS EVER KNOWN,** IN FRONT OF THIS VENT.

AS USUAL.

≥CLICK!≤

NIGHTY NIGHT!

ZAT DEVIOUS SKUNK!

HE KNOWS I'M HIDING IN ZE AIR DUCTS!

HE'S TRYING TO LURE ME OUT!

WELL ZIS TIME, IT HAS WORKED. LET US JUST HAVE A QUICK LOOK...

CRE-EEE-EAK!

AH. LE FOX. SO KIND OF YOU TO JOIN US.

CLICK!

ZUT!!

213

215

MONKEY, AS THE NEW CHIEF SCIENCE OFFICER- ...SIGH... AS THE NEW **KING** OF MEANIECORP, YOU CAN USE ANY OF OUR WEAPONS AT ANY TIME.

KING.

BRILLIANT! LET'S GO!

HOWEVER, IT IS IMPORTANT THAT YOU UNDERSTAND HOW THEY **WORK**, FIRST.

·MMM·

HERE AT MEANIECORP, WE STUDY **LIFE**. NATURE'S GLORIOUS BOUNTY OF CREATURES! AND WE USE WHAT WE LEARN FROM THE ANIMAL KINGDOM TO CREATE INCREDIBLE CREATIONS OF DESTRUCTION.

SIR! HE'S IN THE INCREDIBLE CREATION OF DESTRUCTION!

BRUM! BRUM!

I'M IN CHARGE! TOOT TOOT!

ARGH!

I'M REALLY NOT SURE WHY **FUTURE-ME** SENT YOU BACK HERE TO TAKE CHARGE.

I'M GOING TO TAKE OVER THE WORLD!

YES, WELL, I SUPPOSE IF THAT'S TRUE, THEN THIS IS THE BEST PLACE TO DO IT FROM.

VERY WELL! PICK AN INVENTION, AND UNLEASH HELL!

OOH... UMM..

EENY... MEANIE... MINE-Y..

HOVER PANDA

GOO-O-TRON

SPIKE-O

EXOSKELETON

BOX 'O' BOMBS

220

"ONWARDS TO SKUNKY"

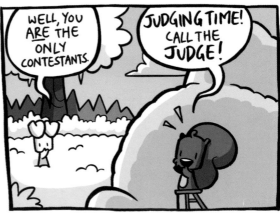

226

227

"THE MONSTROUS BELOW"

YOU **MUST** HAVE. STRANGE THINGS ARE HAPPENING OUT IN ZE WOODS!

PIG AND WEENIE DON'T EVEN REMEMBER WHATSISNAME ANY MORE.

WHO?

SEE?!

LOOK AT MY **PAW**, SKUNKY. IT HAS BEEN SLOWLY DISAPPEARING...

JUST LIKE PIG'S **NOSE**... AND BUNNY'S **EAR**...

MY WHAT ... AUGH!

SKUNKY, YOUR WEAPON. WHAT DOES IT ACTUALLY **DO**?

IT'S A **REALITY DISCOMBOBULATOR** IT BENDS SPACE AND TIME, WARPING DIMENSIONS!

SO THIS **IS** YOUR FAULT!

IT CAN'T BE! I HAVEN'T WORKED OUT HOW TO TURN IT **ON**.

229

HAVE YOU NOT NOTICED ANY WEIRD THINGS HAPPENING?

WELL, MONKEY DISAPPEARED. THAT WAS WEIRD. AND EVER SINCE THEN, THERE'S BEEN THIS STRANGE RUMBLING UNDERNEATH THE GROUND.

RUMMMMBLE!!

THERE IT IS AGAIN! I THINK THE TOILETS ARE BACKING UP!

SHRIEK!

SKUNKY, IT MIGHT BE CONNECTED TO ALL THIS! WE HAVE TO FIND OUT WHAT'S DOWN THERE!

OKAY! OKAY!

I WILL COME WITH YOU. I CAN...

NO, LE FOX. TAKE PIG AND WEENIE FAR AWAY FROM HERE!

BOO HOO!

BUT... I AM ZE PROTECTOR OF ZE WOODS!

IT IS MY DUTY TO FIX ZIS...

ONE OF US HAS WET OURSELF!

WELL, ALL THE PLUMBING LEADS DOWN HERE..

I'VE NEVER DARED GO THIS FAR, THOUGH.

TOO CREEPY!

RUMMMBLE!

NYAHHH!

GOOD IDEA! YOU GO FIRST!

I CAN'T SEE ANYTHING! IT'S TOO DARK!

BUNNY?

BUNNY? IS THAT YOU?

GAAAASP!

MONKEY! HOW LONG HAVE YOU BEEN DOWN HERE?

BUNNY, I WORKED IT OUT!

IT'S NOT THE MOSHOGGOTH AFFECTING REALITY, OR MY DEVICE. IT'S **MONKEY!** HE'S AN **ANOMALY!**

AN ANOMAWHATTY?

HE'S ONLY BEEN MISSING A LITTLE WHILE TO US, BUT IT HAS BEEN **YEARS** TO HIM. SOMEONE MUST HAVE **SENT HIM BACK IN TIME.** HE SHOULDN'T **EXIST** HERE!

THEN WHAT DO WE DO?

WE TRY AND GET MY COMBOBULATOR WORKING, IN THE HOPE IT CAN BEND TIME AND SPACE...

SHAKE! SHAKE! SHAKE!

TO BRING MONKEY **BACK FROM THE PAST!**

BWOOP!

WELL, I'LL JUST STAY HERE THEN, SHALL I?

234

FANTASTIC LE FOX

TEN YEARS AGO...

MY NAME IS LE FOX.

I AM ZE PROTECTOR OF THESE WOODS.

IF ANY CREATURE SHOULD TRY TO DESTROY OUR WORLD, I WILL FIGHT WITH TOOTH AND CLAW.

WHATEVER ZE COST.

BUT LET US GO BACK JUST A FEW MOMENTS MORE...

ARGH! YOU'VE TRANSPORTED US BACK IN TIME TO WHEN THE MOSHOGGOTH WAS **FIRST** RELEASED!

EXCELLENT! IF WE CAN FIND MONKEY HERE IN THE PAST, THEN WE CAN TAKE HIM **BACK TO THE FUTURE!** ...AND **RESTORE** THE **TIMELINE!**

MY REALITY DISCOMBOBULATOR!

DON'T WE NEED THAT?

YOINK!

YES!

WITHOUT IT, WE CAN'T REALIGN THE TIMELINES.

AND IF WE CAN'T DO THAT...

...WE'LL DISAPPEAR FOREVER!

(ZIS IS ME HIDING IN ZE CRATE, BY ZE WAY. I COULD NOT RISK BUNNY AND SKUNKY MESSING ZIS UP ON THEIR OWN)

HOWEVER, THEIR STORY IS MORE IMPORTANT RIGHT NOW...

EVACUATE! EVACUATE MEANIECORP!

HANG ON, IS THAT...?

NO TIME! WE HAVE TO KEEP GOING!

237

EXCELLENT PLAN, BUNNY! GET IT TO TAKE YOU UP THERE!

NOT A PLAN!

NOT A PLAN!

I CAN SEE THE REALITY DISCOMBOBULATOR!

GOOD! NOW GRAB IT, AND LET'S GET OUT OF HERE!

BUT WHAT ABOUT MONKEY?!

YEAH, I'VE BEEN THINKING ABOUT THAT. EVEN IF WE DID SAVE HIM...

...THIS MONSTER'S OUT NOW, AND ABOUT TO DESTROY THE WORLD!

SO LET'S JUST USE MY DEVICE TO TRAVEL TO MARS OR SOMETHING, INSTEAD!

AARGH! I'VE FOUND ITS MOUTH!

I DIDN'T MEAN TO!

AH STOP WHINING, YOU BIG SISSY!

BOOF!

352!

GAH! NOW HOW ARE WE SUPPOSED TO GET THE DISCOMBOBULATOR?

WE COULD HAVE ESCAPED!

241

THE REALITY DISCOMBOBULATOR!

HE'S USING IT TO TRANSPORT THE MOSHOGGOTH OUT OF **REALITY ITSELF!!**

BUT IT'LL TAKE HIM WITH IT!

AND THE WHOLE MEANIECORP BUILDING AT THIS RATE.

GASP! THERE HE IS. MONKEY!

WHAT ARE THEY DOING TO HIM?

WE'VE WIPED HIS BRAIN, SIR. HE WON'T REMEMBER A THING.
GOOD. GOOD.
POP!
FRRP!
NOW LET US FIRE HIM INTO SPACE, SO NO ONE WILL EVER KNOW WHAT TERRIBLE MISTAKES WE MADE.
FWOOSH!!
AND WE CAN ESCAPE IN OUR TIME MACHINE...
HOI!
SORRY! BORROWING IT!
BWOOOOZOOOOOOP!!
FIRING MONKEY INTO SPACE COMPLETED THE LOOP. HE CRASH-LANDED INTO THE WOODS, AS BEFORE, AND THE TIMELINE WAS RESTORED.
WHAT STRANGE PLANET IS THIS?
UPON THEIR RETURN TO THE PRESENT, BUNNY, SKUNKY AND THEIR NEW FRIEND SAW ONLY AN EMPTY SPACE WHERE THE MEANIECORP LABS ONCE WERE.
WHERE I ONCE WAS.
JAMIE
I DID MY DUTY. I SAVED THE WOODS.
MY NAME WAS LE FOX.

"REMEMBERING FRIENDS"

IT'S STILL IN ONE PIECE!

MY HIDDEN CORNER OF MEANIECORP!

MY LAB!

MY BEAUTIFUL, BEAUTIFUL LAB!

AW, SHAME.

MY **ANNIHILATOR!** MY **SMASHYOVERDRIVEÁTRON!** I'M SO SORRY I LEFT YOU.

MWAH! MWAH!

KISS KISS!

UGH!

EXCELLENT NEWS! LET US RESUME OUR HAVOC WREAKING IMMEDIATELY, SKUNKY!

WHAT? WHY SHOULD I TAKE ORDERS FROM YOU?

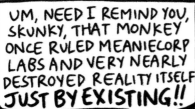

UM, NEED I REMIND YOU, SKUNKY, THAT MONKEY ONCE RULED MEANIECORP LABS AND VERY NEARLY DESTROYED REALITY ITSELF JUST BY EXISTING!!

IT COULD BE ARGUED THAT, PURELY BY ACCIDENT, HE'S THE MOST DANGEROUS MONKEY ALIVE!

I DID WHAT?

YOU MIGHT BE WISER TO KEEP HIM CLOSE, THAN ANNOY HIM.

FINE. FINE! WHAT SHALL WE INVENT FIRST THEN, MONKEY?

A GIANT MECHANICAL SAUSAGE!!

MAYBE I'LL LEAVE YOU TWO TO IT.

ABOVE GROUND...

OH! HEY, IS THAT THE SKUNK'S SECRET LAIR?

YEAH. LOOKS LIKE HE'S BACK IN ACTION.

THESE WOODS MIGHT GET A LITTLE...CRAZY AGAIN.

BRILLIANT! I LOVE CRAZY!

YOU DO? WELL, WOULD YOU WANT TO HANG AROUND? WE COULD SURE DO WITH THE HELP, NOW LE FOX IS...GONE.

245

I'D LOVE TO! MY NAME IS AI!

IT'S SHORT FOR AYE-AYE!

WHAT'S AN AYE-AYE?

I-I AM!

HEH.

SHAKEY-SHAKE!

I'M SORRY ABOUT YOUR FOX FRIEND, BY THE WAY. THE WAY HE TOOK DOWN THAT MOSHOGGOTH THOUGH - AMAZING!

YEAH. HE WAS A REAL HERO.

THEN WE MUST **REMEMBER** HIM. LIKE, **PROPERLY!**

WHAT DO YOU MEAN?

BUILD SOMETHING TO HONOUR HIM!

WHAT A GREAT IDEA! AND I KNOW JUST WHO WOULD WANT TO BUILD IT!

QUITE SOME TIME LATER...

WE'VE DONE IT, BUNNY! MOST OF LE FOX'S HEAD IS HEDGE, BUT WE HID SOME CAKES IN IT SO BIRDS WOULD SIT ON HIM.

I'M SURE LE FOX WOULD LOVE IT!

NO, HE WOULDN'T. HE'D BE VERY VERY GRUMPY ABOUT IT.

AND THAT'S EXACTLY HOW I THINK HE'D WANT TO BE REMEMBERED.

CLANG! CLANG! CLANG!

THE END!

HOW TO DRAW

ACTION BEAVER

OUT OF ALL THE BUNNY VS MONKEY CHARACTERS, **ACTION BEAVER** CAN OFTEN BE THE HARDEST TO DRAW! BUT IF YOU THINK YOU'RE UP FOR THE CHALLENGE, HERE ARE A FEW HELPFUL TIPS...

①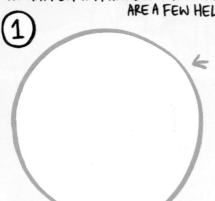

WE'RE GOING TO USE A PENCIL FIRST TO HELP US POSITION EVERYTHING PROPERLY, SO **DRAW A CIRCLE** FOR ACTION BEAVER'S HEAD.

②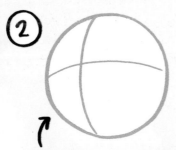

OFTEN WE USE A CROSS TO WORK OUT THE FACE, BUT THIS TIME **CURVE THE CROSS** SO THAT IT BULGES OUT A BIT.

③

THE HORIZONTAL LINE OF THAT CROSS IS THE BASE OF ACTION BEAVER'S **VISOR**. DRAW ANOTHER CURVED LINE TO FINISH IT.

④

LET'S TAKE THIS CHANCE TO DRAW ACTION BEAVER'S FACE... FIRST, A **NOSE!**

⑤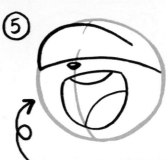

THEN A WIDE OPEN HAPPY **MOUTH!**

⑥

AND DON'T FORGET THE TUFT OF CHEEK HAIR!

⑦

NEXT, WE NEED TO DRAW THE REST OF THE **HELMET.** IT'S BASICALLY ANOTHER CIRCLE, BUT IT CAN TAKE PRACTICE TO GET IT IN THE RIGHT PLACE.

⑧

ACTION BEAVER'S HELMET HAS STRIPES AT THE TOP. WE CAN SHOW THESE WITH CURVED LINES.

⑨

AND DON'T FORGET THE **CRACK** IN THE TOP RIGHT CORNER!

① ACTION BEAVER'S BODY IS A LUMP, BUT LET'S DRAW HIM **RUNNING!**

② ADD CIRCLES FOR HIS **FEET,** ONE OUT IN FRONT, ONE BEHIND.

③ DRAW SOME SAUSAGES FOR **ARMS,** THEN ADD **FINGERS!**

④ DON'T FORGET THE **TAIL,** AND A CIRCLE OF BELLY FUR!

AND THERE WE HAVE IT, **ACTION BEAVER,** BARELY ESCAPING ANOTHER CALAMITY! THINK ABOUT WHAT SORT OF CHAOS HE MIGHT BE INVOLVED IN, THEN TRY DRAWING HIM FLINGING HIMSELF INTO THE MIDDLE OF IT ALL!

BOOM!!

①

LE FOX HAS THE SAME SHAPE OF HEAD AS A LOT OF BUNNY VS MONKEY CHARACTERS DO. IT'S LIKE A **BULGING SQUARE!**

NEXT, WE NEED TO DRAW HIS **FACE** ONTO IT!

②

TRY DRAWING A CROSS IN PENCIL, IT'LL HELP YOU TO THINK ABOUT WHERE LE FOX'S **FACE** WILL FIT ONTO HIS **HEAD!**

③

THEN THE FIRST THING WE DRAW IS LE FOX'S **EYEBROWS!** THEY'RE A STRANGE SHAPE, TRY AND COPY THIS ONE!

(4)

SAME SHAPE, BUT FLIPPED, FOR THE OTHER EYEBROW!

(5)

THEN A LINE UNDER EACH. THIS SHOWS LE FOX IS LOOKING VERY GRUMPY!

(6)

A SNOUT NEXT, COMING OUT JUST BELOW HIS EYEBROWS...

(7)

ADD A LITTLE TRIANGULAR **NOSE** AND AN UPTURNED **MOUTH!**

(8)

FOR THE FUR AROUND HIS FACE DRAW THIS SHAPE (DON'T FORGET THE TUFT FOR HIS **CHEEK!**).

(9)

... ADD THE LAST COUPLE OF **TUFTS**...

ALSO...
LE FOX'S **EARS** ARE THIS SHAPE → AND THEY GO ON THE VERY TOP OF HIS HEAD.

A NOTE ABOUT LE FOX'S **EXPRESSIONS**:
LE FOX USUALLY HAS ONE EMOTION: **GRUMPY!**
BUT WE CAN STILL VARY THAT UP A BIT, TRY
PLAYING AROUND WITH HIS MOUTH TO SEE
JUST HOW GRUMPY LE FOX CAN BE!

ANGRY
GRUMPY

CURIOUS
GRUMPY

SHOCKED
GRUMPY

CONFUSED
GRUMPY

①

LE FOX'S BODY IS JUST
LIKE EVERY OTHER BVM
CHARACTER... A **LUMP!**

②

HIS **ARMS** ARE LIKE
SAUSAGES (ADD FINGERS
AT THE VERY END!)

③

THE ARMS CAN BE
SHAPED INTO ANY
POSITION YOU LIKE!

④

ADD A BIG
BUSHY TAIL.

ADD A CIRCLE
FOR THE TUMMY
FUR.

AND THERE WE HAVE IT, A THOROUGHLY
GRUMPY **LE FOX!** TRY PLAYING AROUND
WITH HIS FACE, HIS ARMS, SEE WHAT
YOU CAN MAKE HIM DO
(BESIDES BEING GRUMPY).

PHOTO BY STEVE BROWN

JAMIE SMART HAS BEEN CREATING CHILDREN'S COMICS FOR MANY YEARS, WITH POPULAR TITLES INCLUDING *BUNNY VS MONKEY*, *LOOSHKIN* AND *FISH-HEAD STEVE*, WHICH BECAME THE FIRST WORK OF ITS KIND TO BE SHORTLISTED FOR THE ROALD DAHL FUNNY PRIZE.

THE FIRST TWO BOOKS IN HIS *FLEMBER* SERIES OF ILLUSTRATED NOVELS ARE AVAILABLE NOW. HE ALSO WORKS ON MULTIMEDIA PROJECTS LIKE *FIND CHAFFY*.

JAMIE LIVES IN THE SOUTH-EAST OF ENGLAND, WHERE HE SPENDS HIS TIME THINKING UP STORIES AND GETTING LOST ON DOG WALKS.